Library of
Davidson College

Songs of my Heart

the Chinese lyric poetry of Ruan Ji (AD 210-263)

*dedicated to
Professor Li Xie*

Wellsweep Chinese Poets 1

Ruan Ji

Songs of my Heart

the Chinese lyric poetry of Ruan Ji

translated by
Graham Hartill
&
Wu Fusheng

Wellsweep

ACKNOWLEDGMENTS

Some of these translations have previously appeared in the magazine *Figs* and *Cabaret 246*.

Artwork for the covers is reproduced from torn paper collages by Bronwyn Borrow designed to illustrate the original poem corresponding to number 35 in this collection.

Copyright © Graham Hartill & Wu Fusheng 1988
All rights reserved

ISBN: 0 948454 00 8

First published in 1988 by
Wellsweep Press
26 Teesdale Road
Leytonstone
London E11 1NQ

Set by Wellsweep
and printed at the Newnorth Press, London E11

Preface

As well as poet, Ruan Ji was soldier, sage, musician and lover of wine. A number of these masks were forced upon him by the circumstances of his times. He was born into the dangerous beginnings of the long period of disunity in China which followed the break up of the Han empire. Where once a talented young man might have expected steady advancement in the military or civil branches of government, he was then faced with perilous – possibly fatal – choices of allegiance between ambitious factions. The result was that Ruan Ji, in common with many others like him, chose instead to live a life of relative disengagement. After a brief military career, wryly commented upon in a number of his poems, Ruan Ji himself turned to wine, music and the philosophical consolations of Daoism.

The surviving biographical material about him contains stories of how he stayed drunk in order to avoid potentially incriminating contacts with the agents of powerful new political forces, out to enlist his services. Whereas under an earlier, more stable regime Ruan Ji might have remained faithful to the worldly ethics of Confucianism (which undoubtedly attracted him), he turned instead to the escapist 'pure conversation' which dominated the philosophical world of the time. He became associated with a group led by his friend Xi Kang (AD 223-262) and known as the 'Seven Sages of the Bamboo Grove'. The worthies of the grove drank and entertained one another, cultivating a reputation for mildly shocking eccentricity and iconoclasm. Xi Kang, their chief, was unambiguously Daoist, a follower of the radical relativism – contemptuous of society's 'dusty world' – which had been handed down in a tradition stemming from writings attributed to Laozi (6th century BC) and Zhuangzi (4th century BC). He was also a dabbler in the associated magico-hygienic practices aimed at procuring winged immortality for the successful adept. Both these strains of Daoism inspire many of Ruan Ji's lyrics and his few remaining prose works include essays and rhapsodic commentaries on the writings of the Daoist philosophical forefathers. As for music, apart from his study of the Chinese zither, Ruan Ji was known for his 'whistling' (*xiao* in Chinese). This was clearly something more than just making a tune by blowing through lips and teeth, since one of the odder stories concerning Ruan Ji describes a whistling contest which he lost to a reclusive 'True Man' on Sumen mountain. Ruan Ji was a fine performer, but whistled himself out when faced with a hidden immortal who then left him with nothing but echoes of the other-worldly music of his vital breath.

As a poet, Ruan Ji is important because of the crucial position of his 'Songs' in the history of Chinese poetry. They were key texts in the development of the poetic forms which came to dominate the golden age of Chinese poetry in the Tang dynasty (AD 618-906). The latter was the period of China's most famous poets, Li Bo and Du Fu, both of whom knew and admired Ruan Ji's work. There were two main reasons for Ruan Ji's influence: because he turned away from the traditional themes of the dominant lyric poetry of the time, concentrating more on individual concerns; and because he helped to advance the progress of a formal pattern for poetry – based on the five syllable line – which was to become the preferred form of traditional Chinese verse, right down to the present day, in so far as it is still practiced.

Traditional Chinese poetry is highly disciplined and Ruan Ji's work is no exception, representing, as it does, an advance in formal poetic practice. It is virtually impossible to translate this aspect of Chinese poetry into English, although experiments can be attempted. The versions in this book are free of formal constraints and are, moreover, free verse in English. Nonetheless, it is still possible to recognize certain features of the originals in these versions, namely their couplet-based structure and the tight parallelism or antithesis of grammar and sense in linked lines.

The accepted view of Ruan Ji's 'Songs of my Heart' is that they are full of obscure allegorical allusions to the political events of his life and times. Much effort has been expended by later critics and commentators in trying – often unsuccessfully – to unravel these obscurities. Such an approach fails to do justice to the work as poetry. The poems are clear, and intensely moving as they stand. Uninterpreted as to their allegorical significance, the literal meanings of the allusive images still stir the imagination and emotion, even across cultures. The aim of this book of versions is to provide an uncluttered view of the originals, as writing which has engaged the work of a young English poet and his Chinese collaborator. These are not scholarly translations, although Wu Fusheng has made use of the existing Chinese scholarship of Ruan Ji. These translations are literary, but free and relatively informal. They are more faithful than adaptations, but far from literal ('mistakes' are intentional). Their aim is to provide the first complete English translation of 'Songs of my Heart' which can be enjoyed as verse.

JHC

Contents

Preface   5

Songs of my Heart   10

Notes   93

General Notes   95

Songs
of
my
Heart

1

Midnight, and I can't sleep.
Sitting up, I play upon my harp.

My gauze curtains mirror the moonlight,
fresh breeze, fluttering my sleeves.

Listen, the lone swan cries, crossing the wilderness,
shriek from the Northern Wood.

Pacing the courtyard, pacing the courtyard,
what can I see?

Anxieties, fretting my heart.

2

Two fairy-girls playing along the riverbank,
lightly, leisurely, hanging on the wind....

They gave their beautiful jewellery to Jiaofu,
how he treasured its fragrance!

Soon Jiaofu and the maidens fell deeply in love
and swore they would never forget one another.
These girls, they were so lovely
the whole town fell on its knees before them!

Alas!
      Their love, and their gratitude, turned to anxiety.
Soon they were planting forgetful grass before their
                              chambers.

So what's the use of putting on make-up?
The rain complains of the morning sun.

Gold-stone and companionship –
why do they both dissolve?

3

I walk the paths under the trees
in the Eastern Garden – peaches, plum trees,
bean-leaves flying everywhere, Autumn wind.

From now on, everything withers and dies.

It is that time – thorns sprout in the courtyard –
time to mount my horse, and head for the Western Hills:
when you can't be sure of your own security
how can you care for your wife and children?

Frost thickens the wild grass.
The year grows old – there's no more left to say.

4

The Heavenly Horses come galloping out of the
                              Northwest,
and on they gallop, along the Eastern Road.
   Spring and Autumn come and go, but tell me –
   how can Fortune be retained?

At dawn, the violets shine with dew in the marsh,
the frost clusters, saturating the grass.
He who is young and handsome in the morning
is ugly and old when evening falls.

   Prince Jin, with his flute which sang like a phoenix,
   flew, flew on a crane,
                        to the peak of Immortal Mountain!

   But I am not him, who is forever beautiful.

5

I remember when I was young at heart,
I paid no heed, singing and playing.
Off I went to Xianyang, the capital,
there to tease the women, flirt with the rich.
All this pleasure was still at its height
when suddenly, night-time fell.

Now I return, on horseback,
and gaze across the far reaches of Three Rivers.

Hundreds of *yi* of gold may be wasted –
never mind. We suffer from too much wealth.

Before me the road runs away to the north;
how can I find the way to a warmer place?

6

I've heard that where the recluse Dongling used to live
he planted melons, right up to the city gates,
so thickly, they covered the earth,
mothers and children, clinging together, spilling across
                                        the paths.
The morning sun would dazzle from them so,
that noble guests would come from all over the country
to gather among their brilliant colours.

Alas, the oil-lamp burns, and consumes only itself,
and too much wealth is a burden, bringing disaster.
All my life I have wanted to wear only the most humble
                                        clothes.

7

This sweltering heat will take its leave of us.
June will not want to stay here.

Fragrant trees, heavy with bright leaves,
blue clouds, wandering across the sky....
So the four seasons turn, and turn around,
the Sun and the Moon rise and fall in their turn.

Back and forth I pace the empty courtyard,
nobody but myself to behold my sadness.

I long in the end for happiness, and harmony,
not pain, not separation.

8

The sun is setting, the light lingers on my clothes,
the wind blows round and round the walls.

Birds huddle together against the cold.
    The Zhouzhou needs a mate to hold him when he
                              dips and drinks,
    the Qiongqiong needs another beast to help him feed.

    Men in power! O! they forget their way out of the
                              labyrinth!

How could I strive for vainglorious fame,
weakening my body, depressing my heart?

I'd rather flutter with the sparrow than soar with the
                                    crane:

that great bird may traverse the ocean,
but which is my way home, once I fly out from its heart?

9

I pass through the Eastern Gate
and look northwards, towards Shouyang Mountain:
at its foot, there are two scholars
        picking the Wei plant –
they are recluses, eating the food of defeated dynasties;
at its peak, there are beautiful forests –
when will we see the hour of brightness?

Frost condenses and wets my clothes.
Wind shocks the hills.
Clouds thicken.

I hear the goose, southwards, crying.
The cuckoo's desolate Autumn song.

The tyrant's music was wild, obscene, the dances strange,
before the exile. Songs hovered along the river,
Up and down they drifted with the time,
looking for short-cuts, following narrow lanes.

Where shall I look? I seek Prince Qiao
who flew on clouds over Deng Forest.
Only the art of lengthening life itself
means anything to me.

11

Deeply the Yangtze river flows
through thick forests of maple.

Look! there is a black horse!
The path is strewn with violets!

There is a softness, and a spring in the air
which saddens my heart.

Once there were many talented scholars
who wrote licentious tales to amuse the King of Chu:
Song Yu wrote of a woman who was a 'morning cloud',
and at evening 'travelling rain'....

Now there are full red blossoms,
spreading themselves and smelling sweet –
    they too know how to indulge themselves.

Once there was a yellow sparrow
who thought that it had no predators –

    thinking of him, who can hold back my tears?

12

I climbed high, and looked out across the wilderness:
to the north, the mountains, shadowed with green pines,
birds fly by, one at a time, crying.

The sorrow returns.
My life has been full of anguish.

> I thought about Gentleman Li, in jail,
> who pined for the Eastern Gate.
>
> And Su, for whom the whole of Three Rivers
> was still too small a place.

And me?   I sought only virtue,
and lo, I have been rewarded with virtue.

Why should I complain?

13

Autumn: I know that it's going to be cold,
lying in bed, listening to the cricket sing
the other side of the curtain. I am fearful,
saddened by this little natural thing.

Gently the breeze tugs at my silken sleeves.
The moon is bright, it shines like ice.
I hear the cockerel crow in the tree-top
and order my horse to be saddled. Time to return.

14

Of such high fortune they were,
Anling and Longyang –
bright as peach-flowers, plum-flowers,
light possessed them,
shining, like the light of spring,
flattering, like Autumn frost.

The charms of their looks and their gestures,
the fragrance of their words, their laughter,
holding hands, indulging in their love,
night and day, sharing the same covers.

They wanted to be a pair of lovebirds,
flying,
    wing touched upon wing.

Taking a brush, they wrote their oath, like so.
And thus their love will never be forgotten.

15

Walking along by Peng Lake
my eyes settle on Daliang, the Place of Wei:
big waves flow ceaselessly down the blue river,
the countryside stretches away
where animals' tracks run back and forth
and birds are flying, each with another.

Now it is the middle of October –
the sun and the moon stare into each other's eyes
and the wind blows fiercely from the north
crystallizing the air.

    I am a stranger here, a loner,
    nodding and shaking my head.
    Villains there are, who only look after themselves,
    and gentlemen, acting as gentlemen will.

    So up and down I wander, thin and pale as a ghost;
    mumbling and chanting I write this poem.

16

I sit alone in the empty courtyard.
Where is the man to whom I can bare my heart?
Outside, before me, stretches an endless road,
an empty road – no cart, no horses.

Climbing, I look over China –
vast, so vast, it spreads before me.
One bird only, heading Northwest,
and some little animal, lost, scurrying the other way.

Evening's the time when I miss my friends the most,
for conversation's comfort and relief.

17

The sun's chariot hangs in the Southwest,
the driver hurries it forward to its setting.
Light lingers across the Four Oceans,
suddenly darkness reigns.

In the morning the sun rises at Xianchi and bathes itself,
and at evening the banks of the Meng accept its light,
but who doubts that the poor scholar, enlightened
                                        as he is,
will never revive, once he has passed away?

Look at those peach and plum flowers –
which of them can keep its lustre forever?
The noble man – where can he stand to be free from
                            change?
What a shame that he can't become one with it all.

I stand and admire the pines on Jingshan Mountain.
They comfort my heart.

18

There is a woman in the West
who is as bright as sunlight.
She wears a dress of the finest silk
and jewellery shines from her left, her right.

Her face is a charm, so full of grace,
faintly perfuming the breeze.
Climbing upward, she keeps watch for her loved one,
holding her sleeves, she faces the morning sun.

She hovers, she drifts through the sky,
waving her sleeves, she dances,
flies like the wind, like a cloud, in trance.

Every so often, she glances at me.
but for me this beauty is out of reach.

Left alone, I lament my fate.

19

In my heart I treasure each moment of time –
the sun's chariot will soon descend into darkness.
Waving my sleeves I brandish the long sword
and holding my head aloft, I watch the clouds in their
                                      courses.
Among them I see a black crane,
firm in its will, making its sad sounds.
Once it darts away, into the blue sky,
its cry will be gone forever.

How can I flutter and flap around with the sparrow
playing down there in the courtyard?

Emperor Xia may have ridden a heavenly dragon,
and Kuafu's stick become the Forest of Deng,
but life and death both follow the process of Change.
The sun and the moon have their rising and falling.

The song of the phoenix is like a flute;
Linglun fashioned a bamboo flute to copy the sound;
Prince Jin played, and generations sought his music –
who says the Way is not to be seen?

Ah bluebird, you who bring food for the goddess,
you are the only one who understands my heart.

21

In the Southeast the holy Ye Mountain rises.
From its southern side the Fen River flows.
Six dragons draw a chariot of *qi,* the breath of life,
drawing a curtain of cloud across the heavenly order.

Four or five celestial beings
feast at leisure in the Orchid House –
in sleep, their breathing is pure and harmonious,
at dawn their breath becomes dew and frost.
They bathe in the deep empyrean pool
on which the sun and the bright moon shines.

Easy and carefree they ascend the tower of the spirit,
upward they swim, to heaven.

22

Deep depression makes a knot of the heart.
To be always on edge is a permanent state of shock.
Before your pleasure has reached its height
the sun sets, suddenly red in the West.

Crickets are chirruping under the window
down in the courtyard, an insect
alive for one brief season.

The hearts of men are estranged from each other.
Who understands, or believes my feelings?
I wish I could be a bird in cloud
whose melancholy song is heard through a thousand *li*.

I'll drink Sanzhi, and live forever
beside the gods and goddesses, on Yingzhou Peak.

23

In the morning, I climbed to the hill top.
At sunset, I kept my eyes on the Western Hills.
Thorns covered the wilderness.
Flocks of graceful birds flew by.

> The phoenix, resting, takes its own
> kind for company.
> All of life follows its natural course.
>
> Who can come close to the magical Jianmu tree?
> The Yegan flower displays its elegance.

Don't you see the vines in the forest,
twined together, all the way up from the root?

24

I would rather face the edge of a drawn sword
than serve in this slanderous court.

The only thing that frightens me is sophistication –
people who try to trap me with their insidious talk –

> The Ethereal Fountain hangs in the Mountain of Jade,
> the sun's chariot stands at rest in the east.
> Thousands of *li* lie between the Sun and the Moon,
> the Autumn winds bring frost.

Yes, the roads of the world roam up and down
but cover no great distance.

25

The Ruo tree illuminates the Chinese land,
the Eastern Forest casts its shadow on Yingzhou Peak.
   The Sun and the Moon cross the sky on their own roads,
     darkness and light never travel together.

Poverty and prosperity also have their ways.
Where should we look to find loss and gain?
How can I imitate those children, there on the road
who run and play with their arms entwined?
Yin and Yang change over, as is their wont.
Who says that if you sink you can never resurface?

The Red River-turtle jumps across the Ethereal Fountain.
The cruel master's sword flies out of his hand
         and comes to earth at Chu.
Sinking, rising, I move with the course of nature
and rest with the flow of the Four Seas.

Burdened with fame and wealth,
the wise and the foolish horses are tied to the self-same
                         cart.

Why not clear my eyes and ears of all of this
and fly away, deserting dejection?

26

There is a place where Zhou and Zheng come
                together under the sky,
and the roads and tracks all run together
                down to Sanhe.
Here the women of grace, the handsome women,
come together, shine like flowers,
dark hair, setting off red faces,
lights in their eyes, tender, alluring.

Women of rarest beauty, come to look at you,
flirt with you; their eyes....
They want to go out in the Spring fields.
The morning sun is already setting.

Rise and fall are only momentary things.

How will we say our farewells?

27

I clambered aboard my cart and left,
                       wishing to travel.
What was the goal of my journey?
The abandonment of vanity and fame.

    For vanity and fame do not rely on you –
      best to follow your innermost heart.
    A single curtain can cut off the sunlight,
      the high pavilion muffles even the deepest tones.

    As calumny separates intimate friends
      floating clouds darken the sky.

Look at that fair, that self-effacing woman,
              giving away her clothes.
A single glance from her and everyone is charmed.

Fortune, favour, come for a moment and go,
never to flourish again.

Morning passes, evening returns.
no-one shares my brooding heart.

O yellow birds! Fly Southeast
and carry these words to a friend.

28

I took a cart, and headed for Daliang,
        the capital of old Wei,
for the South, for the Chui Pavilion,
where the music of the flute still lingers.

Where is the King of Liang?
His soldiers ate chaff for their only food,
and wise men were driven into the wilderness.
Before the songs and the dances had ended
the army of Qin had already appeared.

The Narrow Forest was ours no longer,
the crimson palaces fallen away to dust.

Liang's troops were defeated at Huayang.

He himself has long been ashes.

The morning sun will never be as bright again
and the day grows suddenly dark in the West.
Yet this parting is only a brief moment,
        a nod of the head,
who says it endures Autumn long?

The life of Man is like the dew in the dust.
How long, and how vast, is the Way of Heaven!

The Duke of Qi looked down from the hill –
tears fell down his face like streams crossing.
Confucius stood by the long river,
lamenting time, so swiftly flowing....

What is past I cannot regain,
and what's to come I cannot keep.
I wish that I could climb the Taihua Mountain
and live up there in heaven, among the gods!

The fisherman knew the sufferings of this world,
so, taking a little skiff,
        he drifted along with the current....

Days after evenings

evenings after mornings

the countenance loses its colour,
the spirit weakens of itself.

A fire is raging within my chest –
everything changes thereby, one thing after another.
Universal phenomena have no end
that Man's pitiful wit can ever penetrate.

My only fear is – that in a moment's time
my soul will catch the wind and fly away.

All my life I've been walking on thin ice.

Who could know my anxious heart?

31

Days after mornings

evenings after mornings

the countenance loses its colour
the spirit floats of itself.

Lifting the cup I lament the fate of Chu
and think of my friends in the old days.

    Facing the drink I cannot speak.

I'd like to go and plough in the paddy-field,
Who understands this kind of truth?

Yet, misery, depression are short-lived,
and noble behaviour will damage a humble body.

Why should I fret myself about the 'straight' and
                    'crooked' things,
here, with dragons and snakes for my neighbours?

32

Worldly affairs are completely disordered....

    and it's a great pity that we can't stay long –
        youth passes within an hour,
            the morning dew awaits the sun.

      I wish that I held the sun-cart's reins!
      Then its brilliant light would never pass!

    The stairway to heaven's a difficult climb,
    and there is no bridge to cross the Milky Way....

      Washing my hair by the side of the Yanggu River,
      travelling far to Kunlun Peak –
          there I climb the Heavenly Hills
            to gather the fragrant violets.

The ways of the world are hardly worth competing for....

    Look! How vast the Cosmos!

33

Who says that life is hard?
Life can disappear in leisure:
    in front of my courtyard there stands a feathery,
                              flowery tree –
    standing alone in its shade, I consider the formless
                              cosmos....

Walking up and down I miss my relatives and friends,
and then the day is dark again.

Let those eastward-flying birds carry my message
and comfort my heart.

34

This morning's hour of joy has come,
yet the drizzle moistens the dust.

I wait by the roadside for my beloved
till evening, still she doesn't come.

Human nature teems with sentiments –
they disturb me, how can I console myself?

With sadness in my heart I wipe away the tears.
Who will listen to these miserable words?

35

A dazzling light extends for a thousand *li*,
the turbulent torrent dashes within the enormous valley!
There is the East he bends his bow
and, sword in hand, he stands at the edge of the sky.
Mount Tai's the stone he whets his sword upon,
the Yellow River he takes as the train of his cloak.

Still I consider the gentleman known as Zhuangzi,
and ask: how can either glory or ignominy be relied on?
Throw away the body, throw it away to the desert
after death, its bones to be feast for birds of prey.
Why should I follow that man, that fabulous warrior,
striding hugely, chasing fame and rank.

36

How brave and how generous are those heroes!
Their only will is to strike the entire world.
Driving chariots to the far battlefield
in their hearts they cherished their leader's trust.
They hold their wonderful bows in their hands,
their armour sheds a magnificent glint.
Confronting danger, they care little for their lives –
when they die, their souls spread out in the sky.
These are not cowards, who struggle
        only to save themselves,
they give themselves devotedly to battle.
Their loyalty will be glory for hundreds of generations,
their deeds will make their names well-known,
their fame will be honoured by the world eternally,
their spiritual integrity will never suffer change.

37

The Sky and the Earth originated in Chaos.

The principles of Yin and Yang, dividing, drive
    the motion of the spheres.

        The sun spreads its brilliance,
        the moon its clear light –
          the sun, once set, will return,
          but the life of Man is short as
        dust in wind,
          vanishing,
            and transient as
        clouds,
            perpetually drying up.

Prolonging life is thus my will!
    (and gaining Imperial favour, not my luck at all!)

        Anqi walks the Road of Heaven a thousand years,
        Songzi leaves the world behind.
          Where can I get the wings, that I could
        harness the clouds, and fly around in
            their splendour?

How strange the will of Confucius!

Why would he want to live down here,
    on this ground?

The Heavenly Web covers the wilderness,
the swan folds up her strong wings
and follows the tide, with thousands of common ducks....

The life of a man can never be predicted,
mornings and evenings, the unexpected –

The gods and goddesses apply themselves to prolonging
life:
fostering their will by spiritual means,
they hover between the clouds and the sun
far, far away from the ways of the world.

Fame and glory are not what I treasure,
women and music can never content me.

Those who seek the *elixir vitae* never return.

Even the words of the gods and goddesses cannot be
trusted!
and when I think of this, I find myself transfixed....

39

The Emperor requires good advisers
and to achieve outstanding things, heroic men
                are needed.
How brilliant and handsome the scholars used to be,
and how they prospered, ringing the air in praise
                      of the enlightened emperors.

Yin and Yang have their time of discord,
the sun and moon are not in balance all of the time.
Nature's course is now harmonious, now discordant,
human affairs are often out of control!

        Yuan and Ji hid themselves away in the
                      mountains,
        Laozi became a recluse in the Northwest –
        the truth of Dao is to hold to one's integrity,
        favour and glory are not worth striving for.

            Of those who are not strong in origin
                only a few can see things through
                      to the end.

Yes, the scholars of ancient days were beautiful –
names that will be remembered forever.

40

Together the cranes fly
to the distant ends of the world.
They spread their wings and soar,
crossing thousands of *li* at a glance.
At dawn, they breakfast on manna,
at nightfall they rest on the godly mountain.
They hover among the clouds displaying their
                          self-possession –
is there a web or a snare that could hold them?

Hah! Why should I mix with those country squires
putting their hands on each other's hands,
swearing their pacts?

41

Similar things grow apart as life proceeds –
physical appearances change.

The jade has its home in the high mountain.
Zhiying, the plant of immortality,
        shines in the courtyard.
How magnificently the plum and the peach-tree bloom!
but once a path is trod beneath them they wither.
How can they yearn for the long, wide road?
They can only display their lustre in springtime.

And me?
        No tree green against wind and frost.
but weariness and decay – nothing that lasts forever.

42

The noble orchid, they say, is not worth wearing –
who does it blossom for then, so well?

The lofty bamboo secludes itself in the mountain shades,
the Yegan flower grows before Cengcheng –
    the home of the gods,
and vines cover the valley slopes,
twined together, full of fruit.

    Over-indulgence in joy can damage our spirits,
    while too much sadness hurts our human feelings.

    Since I myself have known the futility of worry,
    why not return to the Great Clearing?

43

The sparrows flit in the forest,
the albatross hangs above the sea

– not that the sparrow is unaware of the sea beyond
but his wings cannot take him there,

unable to glide, or to soar,
better to rest in the twigs.

>   Down below, the sparrows cluster on the grass,
>   look up! they're playing on the fence.
>   Since they are so full of themselves right here,
>   why should they follow that other bird?

The moment of birth is beyond control.
Tears dampen my sleeves.

The eagle glides over the mountain,
the sparrow lingers below in the bushes.
My sighs fill the courtyard like a cloud,
my heart is saddened by this music.

The crane flies, singing, across the peak,

how can we follow him?

45

Tiny birds play and sing on the tree in the courtyard,
a goose glides by on the clouds.

Look at that lonely bird in the sky,
flying, slowly, with no companion....

Life and death depend upon the Law of Nature,
always recurring, fading away, extinction....

46

Walking by the crossroads
with a sad heart, I miss my beloved.

Not that I hope to see her today,
but she comes, from a state of trance she appears....

Before me, on the moor, there stands a giant tree –
no, eternal glory cannot be expected.

Huge birds wheel across the sky,
playing, one with another, among the clouds.

Why be the lonely, wayward scholar,
shedding tears, lamenting the past?

47

The fresh dew congeals into frost,
the luscious grass is overgrown with weeds.

Who can talk about noble virtues,
and how can wisdom and enlightenment endure?

Riding the clouds, I seek the Immortals,
breathing pure air,
               breathing,
                             breathing,
                                       alas!

The loyal heart has lost the favours bestowed on it.
Too much concern with behaviour is harmful.
Fine words, they don't endure,
and royal favour is never easy to come by.

Ah! Don't you see the swallows flying southward,
slowly spreading their wings to the air?

Gaozi complains about plaintive poetry,
but Qu Yuan makes his name from it.
Alas! even Chaos himself was destroyed
by Shu and Hu, who didn't understand his nature.

49

The Ten Suns rise in the East,
their drivers whip them onward, thousands of *li*.
Crossing the sky, they shine down upon China,
suddenly, they sink in the West.

Who says their lustre endures?

That is why the wise man drifts along the river of time.

What is passing cannot remain.
Such are the thorns and thistles of this world.

Thousands of years are just a day.
Life is a dinner-party. Time passes.

Right and wrong, gain and loss –
how can it be worthwhile to vex oneself?

When desire for profit or knowledge come to an end,
so will the sadness of Man.

Nature has its way of doing things,
the course of life and death can never be known.
From wisdom and tact evil and trouble come,
The Way of Nature never changes.

Look at those delicate ladies,
flirting, feigning tender hearts,
who ride in a carriage pulled by the finest steeds,
who sit at a table of jade, and nibble the finest foods,
whose clothes are cut from satin and silk,
whose boudoirs are hidden, deep, deep in the palace –

Don't they see the flowers that bloom in daylight?
falling, one by one, along the side of the road?

51

Boasting and gossiping relieve one's anger,
but laziness only breeds anxiety.
So, I climb up Buzhou mountain, heading Northwest
and I turn and stare: behind me the Forest of Deng,
a great expanse of wilderness, stretching across the land.

The hills are lifted up on the backs of enormous
                              mountains.
An age is spent in the time it takes to eat.

Thousands of years, rising and falling,
who says that jade and rock are of the self-same kind?

Nothing to do to check these tears.

52

People say they wish to prolong their lives.
Having done that, however, where can they go from
                              there?
The yellow crane calls out to its immortal rider.
Eternal life can never be expected.

Alone, I sit among the mountain rocks.
My heart is sore, and misses my beloved.
I wonder what the Immortals yearn for?
Intimate love and harmony between each other.

Beauty passes away as this morning passes away,
indulgence in fame and wealth is only
                a moment's pleasure.

Give up any thoughts about tomorrow.
This very evening we will find ourselves deceived.

53

Illustriousness and lowliness – both are in the hands
                of Providence:
the wealthy and poor, both must pursue
                their own courses.
Young and handsome, vile and mean,
ensnare each other to gain advantage.
Perseverance in truth is a lonely business:
you lose favour at court, and the sycophants slander
                and scorn you.

The Eagles sing in the clouds!
They soar and they hover, with nothing to hope for.

Those of you who depend on rich and powerful men,
don't you know that when your patrons fall,
you too will be dragged down?

54

The tempest strikes the wild earth,
flying clouds darken the courtyard.

For whom is the bed-curtain hung?
Who will use the walking-stick and the table?

Though I'm not gifted myself with uncanny sight,
still my vision can penetrate the darkening West:

the world is filled with the deaf and the dumb,
where can I go in this vast country?

> I want to fly with a light heart, in the wind,
> far, far away from this my native land,
> until I arrive at the Jade Mountain,
> leaving all slander, and all promotion,
> abandoned....

55

My high hat divides the floating clouds,
my sword stretches out to the edge of the sky.

The trifles of this world are no concern of mine,
I stand on high to overlook all this.
    Mounting my steed I will gallop away
    and wander in the wilderness with an easy heart.

I bid farewell to Xiwangmu the goddess.
The goal of my journey is still to be reached.

    How could I mix with these narrow-minded recluses,
    playing their harps and singing, swearing their oaths?

56

By the side of this river there lived a man
who, though he was poor, threw the ruby away.
Simple food was delicious to him,
and comfortable to him his shabby shelter.

Why should we bustle along with the noisy crowd,
the fine horses, heaving luxurious carriages?
Born in the morning along the avenue –
buried at night on some street corner.
Even before their laughter has faded,
sighs and moaning arise to replace it.

Instructed by these people's fate,
the anger in my heart is liberated.

57

The Confucianists are well-versed in the Six Classics,
no-one can shake their tenacious will.
They never act in discord with the rituals,
they'll never speak against the rules.
Thirsty, they drink from clear fountains,
hungry, they eat from bamboo bowls.
When times of sacrifice come, they can offer nothing,
their shabby clothes can barely protect them against
                              the cold –
but on they go, in worn-out shoes, chanting their verses,
acting with ease and confidence in elegant houses.
Loyal to their beliefs they live among books,
refusing handouts for justice's sake.

For this, they are both praised and vilified –

    Laozi sighed....

When young, I learned the Dance of Swords.
My skill surpassed even the Master of Qu.
My spirit was heroic! Cutting the sky!
My fame spread wide in the world.

I brandished my sword in the desert battlefield,
my horse drank in the wilderness.
O! the banners, flying against the wind!
The racket of drum-beats!

But military matters depress me now,
thinking back on my former years,
when all my bitterness was born.

59

Dressing up at midday,
I long to meet a guest.

Who is this guest?

He is as uncertain as the flying dust,
clouds and air are his clothes,
gods and goddesses his topic.

He leaves at a glance.

Where can I meet this character?

Too many worries unfocus one's will,
loneliness harasses the heart.

I wander away, and stare at the marsh where
                my loved one lives,
and, grasping my sword, set foot on a light canoe.

Ah, I hope that the rest of my life will be
                as easy-hearted as this,
that I may return in years to come.

61

When morning came, I walked out from the Eastern Gate
and gazed across at Shouyang Mount in the distance –
that place where the faithful sons escaped to after the
overthrow.

Dense pines cast deep shadows across its face
and orioles played, one with another.

Strolling among the meandering streams,
haltingly, unsure of my direction,
all the routine of my everyday life came into my mind.

I thought about that beautiful girl,
the concubine of the last tyrant of Shang.

62

This prince was fifteen years of age
when he travelled along the Yi and Luo Rivers.
His face was blooming and red as a spring flower,
his wit was quick and his heart innocent.

But was there a place for him to encounter the
      Gentleman Fou
and thus to bid farewell to everyone here for good?
Prince Jin did.
    Lost in trance, forsaking his body,
he drifted away on the wind,
hovering, singing,
and feeling a little sore,
with outstretched wings.

63

Men cannot pass through the polar gate of the north
or stay afloat on the ocean.

Brightness doesn't come to see me,
darkness, only darkness without limit.

Holding a melon in both my hands, my thoughts return
                          to Dongling.
The yellow sparrow makes me feel ashamed.

I think of the starving man in the mulberry grove
                who shared his food
and tear-tracks cross my face.

I'll take a cart, and travel between the rivers,
saddle a horse, and make for distant lands.

The renown of the Confucian scholar
        relies on certain rules:

he dresses according to convention,
a definite line is drawn between the superior
                and inferior,
and every thing, and every act is strictly set.
Every facial gesture, every stroke of make-up,
every piece of jewellery worn at court
                designed to impress.
In their courtyards the ceremonial water is stored,
and the ritual rice in their houses.
In public they put on noble, gracious airs,
within, all the beautiful things are extinguished.
Dissolute talk comes straight from their hearts,
but barely a minute passes
                before they resume their moral rhetoric.

How false and affected all their behaviour,
pretensions and attitudes!
                      I lament them.

65

Northward, I face the Ganmei Valley,
then I travel Westward, without end.

In the far distance I see the Heavenly Ford,
its enormity pleases my heart.

Satiated at the Gate of Life and Death
I travel onward, no longer seeking for anything.
If by chance I meet the Chenfeng Bird, of the wicked
       House of Jin,
I turn in another direction, flying across the Southern
       Forest.

Having merged completely into the whirling cosmos,
I reside there, free, refreshing myself in its wild liberty,
      resting myself in the Pure City.

Who can prevent me rising above this corrupted world?

66

All of us know how hard it is to associate
                with others,
but to make true friends is indeed a difficult thing.
The path of life is dangerous, people grow suspicious,
                the ruby glows beyond our reach.

That man wants to eat the food of kings,
but for me, a bowl of rice is enough –

reducing his share and adding to mine will anger us
                              both,
and any advice, or any suggestion,
just a waste of breath.

67

Man is a creature of sensibility, therefore of sorrow,
but without sorrow there is no consideration.
If traps and snares were not awaiting me,
why should I need to travel so far and wide?

Floating on the wind, I touch the depths of the sky.
The villainous clouds erase the rising sun.

  – Heart like ashes, body like withered trees.

Why should I bother about the affairs of men?

One should leave oneself to silence.
But here I know the difficulty of self-forgetting.

The Mujin flowers blossom on the rolling graves,
these hills are lovely, and luminous.
The radiant sun goes down into the trees
as one by one, the flowers fall.
Outside my window a cricket is singing,
transient thing in the thorn.

Mayflies play for their three days,
their wings are as slender and pretty as feathers.
Who are their costumes designed for?
To decorate their little moment.

The life of Man is also brief.
Our hearts know it. We should
      try our best to live.

69

The long trail is appropriate for the carriage,
the river, wide and long, bears up the light boat.

How can life be determined by nature's course
when fame and wealth so affect our desires?
This longing for fame confuses the will,
and for riches, worries the heart.

Friends act inconsistently towards one another
and people of self-same blood become
                each other's enemies.

I wish that all the pearls, and all the rubies in the world
                could be done away with,
then we could roam, and climb the mountains, easy,
                buoyant-hearted.

70

Behold at the cross-ways there stands an outstanding
                              man,
a chestnut steed to pull his chariot!

When morning rises, he sets out from the mountain of
                              the gods,
and at evening he rests, where brightness reigns forever.

Next time you see him
    he's left these lands,
his wings spread.

Yes, I will leave all the things of this world behind!
Why should I let all this trivia pester my heart?

Let a thousand years pass –
we'll meet again.

71

O, the scholars of bygone days,
indifferent to ambition, living the simple life!
In this degenerate world, truth declines –
people rush here and there, everywhere dirt and dust.

Who can say that Ning Qi is ignoble?
Who can hear Yang Zhu's song and still wish for
                                        martyrdom?

Restless people are not my companions,
people who bustle and rush are not my type.

Glory and shame can change in a moment.
Coming and going I feel the truth of Dao.

The truth of Dao is indeed a pleasant thing –
in innocence and purity the spirit is retained.

Chao and You are both noble characters.

From now on, I too will go down to the riverside.

72

At Liangdong, fragrant flowers grow
which blossom many times in a single day.
Lovely their faces, gestures, charming,
shining through the town.

But how can a man like me grow wise,
seduction and flattery rising up,
and dandyism, frivolity, gone in a moment?

How can they know the kind of name that endures
                    forever?

Fair ones! at the end of the road,
fearful of sunset, moonset,
can't you see the Mingling tree?

It loses its shape in the vastness of space.

73

How can you learn to ride as fast as flying?
Dongye, who over-used his horses, lost his wits
             by the roadside!

Fish swim in the deep water below the hook,
birds fly high above the trap –

I will take a light boat, and float downstream
to where there is nothing to see but endless water.

What good is it, to moisten each other after we're
                              beached?
Better forgetting each other in river or lake.

It's a difficult thing to be fair of face –
just to keep myself clean is enough for me.

Longevity belongs to the gods and goddesses,
living in endless trance.

74

In a moment of time old age arrives,
a mere nod of the head. Yet always worry,
          always anxiety!

I stand by the side of rivers, envying their ceaseless
                      motion,
out from a single source dividing.
A hundred years. It's hardly worth talking about!
Hatred and complaint harass me.

Who are these people, hating and complaining?
Even the eyes and the ears scorn one another,
sound and colour – distinct as North and South!
Even human feelings persecute each other.

How I long to meet that scholar, who's so well-versed
        in the truth of things
that he comes and goes forever, strolling along
        with the course of nature.

75

Once upon a time, there were gods and goddesses
                living on Ye Mountain.
Riding dragons, flying on clouds,
they breathed immortal air, they ate ambrosia.
They could be heard, but they couldn't be seen –
                how I am moved by this!

Firstly, I lament my fate for not being one of their caste,
then, distress and anxiety come, to add themselves to
                my state.

"I studied below, but my learning penetrates heaven."

Suddenly, the times have changed.
    Where should I head for now?

76

In the forest there dwells an extraordinary bird
                known as a phoenix.
Mornings he drinks from the clear fountain,
evenings he rests on the mountaintop.
He sings at the top of his voice across the Four Oceans,
he stretches his neck and peers about him across the
                wilderness.
When the villainous Autumn winds begin to blow
                and crack his wings,
he flies to the western side of Kunlun Mountain.
No-one knows the time of his return.

But no, I am not like him.
My heart breaks.

77

Walking through the Eastern Gate I gaze around
    for my beloved.

Is my beloved here?

The mountains themselves are godlike, attracting
    gods and goddesses.

Who can expect eternal life?

Life and death are long and short –
what can I know from this?

The morning sun sets suddenly –
moving, moving, which way should I take?

Don't you see the Autumn grass and trees?

Even now they're broken up for firewood.

78

Once upon a time those gods
called Xianmen, Song and Qiao
lived in state at the edge of the sky.
They climbed up into heaven to take their food.

Man yearns for a long life,
a hundred years is far, far away.

Evening never turns to morning.

So much better to leave all worldly things behind
and move as freely, unfettered as stars in heaven.

79

The Mujin flowers blossom, shine,
      before the graves.
Their charm, their beauty, is not perfected
before they're shattered by ceaseless wind,
      the ceaseless rain....

How can they be compared with Langgan and Danhe,
which grow like grass on the Western Mount?
They stand on the high cliffs and cast shadows,
their light lingers upon the land.

Youth sighs,
the day passes....

Years ago, at fourteen and fifteen,
with high ambition I fell in love with poetry and books.
I wore the simplest clothes, but in my heart, I cherished
        the ruby and pearl,
setting Yan Hui and Min Sun up as my models.

In an open cart I turned my face to the wide fields,
climbing ever upward I sought to follow my heroes.

The mounds of graves cover the hillsides,
thousands of years have passed in a single moment,
thousands of Autumns, tens of thousands of years –

Now I know the truth of the Immortals,
and laugh at myself, my rolling tears.

81

>
> Yang Zhu wept, facing the crossroads.
> Mozi grieved, the silk was white,
> and fading.

The custom of yielding the throne to virtue has not been
>
> seen for a long time.
What can you expect in these stormy, turbulent days?
How come these usurpers can seem so devoted?
The country's fate is determined by seeing
>
> the real truth of things.

Desertion brings the people sorrow.
Misfortune cannot be refused.

The King of Dai, who was charmed by the girl of Chao,
was made a fool by tenderness and modesty.

O, I think of the common scholars, treading along their
>
> roads.
Where can they find their peace and safety?

82

Once, I travelled to Daliang,
and climbed to the top of Huanghua Mountain.

The dwelling place of Gonggong was gloomy and deep,
with its platform rising, rising into the blue....

   A dim, O such a remote, an untamed place....
   and sorrow fell, as someone dear to me came into
              my heart.

   Who was this beloved man?

                An enlightened mind should follow the
                       course of nature.

          The Dragon Ying, the Dragon of Flood
                            dived deep
      into the waters at Jizhou,
      and Nüwa, the Goddess of Drought,
          could rest there no longer.

Stubborn in his mind, extravagant in life, he
        trespassed far from normality.
Alas, he cannot be said to have lengthened life.

Notes

While wishing to avoid detailed discussion of the hundreds of references to name, place, creature and plant in these poems, there are a number of occasions where some illumination may be useful.

Poem 48 makes reference to a fable in the *Book of Zhuangzi*. Close-by the sea-gods, Shu and Hu, dwelt Chaos. Shu and Hu would get together in the realm of Chaos, who was always the perfect host. In an attempt to show their gratitude for his hospitality they decided to reward him with the seven apertures common to other beings – two eyes, two ears, two nostrils and a mouth. This they did, at the rate of one a day. By the seventh day poor Chaos – now ordered by the senses – was no more.

In **Poem 54** the allusion to the bed-curtain comes from the *Han shu* (an official history of the Han dynasty). There it is noted that when a certain Rong Heng fell ill, the Emperor himself paid him a visit and made him a gift of a bed-curtain. In the *Li ji* it is said that when a man of seventy still holds an official position he should be awarded a walking-stick and a table as a mark of respect.

Poem 62 draws on a legendary tale about Prince Jin. It is said that at the age of 15, while travelling along the Yi and Luo Rivers, he met with Fuqiu who was versed in the ways of immortality. Jin was taken away by Fuqiu and became a god.

In the *Huainanzi* there is a story about Ning Qi, who is referred to in **Poem 71**. As a pauper he had no access to the King of Qi but, waiting for a time when guests were visiting the palace, he sang a song of such distinction that he himself was summoned to the gathering. Ning Qi went on to attain a high position in the court. Of further relevance to poem 71, in the *Liezi* there is a tale to the effect that Yang Zhu, a philosopher of the Warring States period, had a friend named Ji Liang who fell dangerously ill. His sons sent for a doctor, and Ji said to Yang, "How foolish my sons are! Why don't you compose a song for me which will help them to understand?". Yang then sang an appropriate ditty, celebrating a fatalistic attitude to blessings and calamities, Life and Death:

"What heaven does not know
How can man discern?
Blessings do not come from heaven,
Nor calamities from the sins of men.
Is it you and I who are ignorant?
Do doctors and shamans understand?"

Ji Liang's sons nonetheless failed to get the point and sent for three doctors, the first usual, the second good, and the third – who recommended allowing the illness to mend itself – 'divine'. Ji Liang's disease did, naturally, cure itself. (translations by A.C. Graham, *The Book of Lieh-tzu*)

Finally, it was Confucius who once said (in *Analects*, XIV.37), "I studied below but my learning penetrates Heaven. Heaven knows me.", as quoted in **Poem 75**.

General Notes

The system of romanization used in this book is Pinyin, now a British Standard as well as the standard of the People's Republic of China. It differs in a number of respects from earlier romanization systems with which some readers may be familiar. The most common of these is Wade-Giles. The following is a table of selected terms occurring in the text with their Wade Giles equivalents, so that identifications can be made.

Pinyin	Wade-Giles	Pinyin	Wade-Giles
Buzhou	Pu-chou	Ruan Ji	Juan Chi
Dai	Tai	Sanhe	San-ho
Daliang	Ta-liang	Sanzhi	San-chih
Dao	Tao	Song Yu	Sung Yü
Daoism	Taoism	Xi Kang	Hsi K'ang
Deng	Teng	Xia	Hsia
Dongling	Tung-ling	Xianchi	Hsien-ch'ih
Du Fu	Tu Fu	Xianmen	Hsien-men
Ganmei	Kan-mei	Xianyang	Hsien-yang
Gaozi	Kao-tzu	Xiwangmu	Hsi-wang-mu
Gonggong	Kung-kung	Yan Hui	Yen Hui
Huainanzi	Huai-nan-tzu	Yang Zhu	Yang Chu
Ji Liang	Chi Liang	Yingzhou	Ying-chou
Jin	Chin	Zheng	Cheng
Jingshan	Ching-shan	Zhiying	Chih-ying
Jizhou	Chi-chou	Zhou	Chou
Laozi	Lao-tzu	Zhuangzi	Chuang-tzu
Li Bo	Li Po		
Liangdong	Liang-tung		
Liezi	Lieh-tzu		
Mozi	Mo-tzu		
Ning Qi	Ning Ch'i		
Nüwa	Nü-wa		
Qi	Ch'i		
Qiao	Ch'iao		
Qin	Ch'in		
Qu	Ch'u		
Qu Yuan	Ch'ü Yüan		

Chinese Text

Chinese texts of the poems in this volume can be obtained by sending a large stamped addressed envelope and one pound sterling to:

>Ruan Ji Chinese Text
>Wellsweep Press
>26 Teesdale Road
>Leytonstone
>London E11 1NQ

The text comes in a paperbound leaflet the same size as the book of translations. It includes a finding list allowing interested readers to match up the poems in the order given in this translation with two of the most recent Chinese editions of Ruan Ji's work.

≈